EX LIBRIS

NAME

ACROSTIC THEOLOGY
FOR KIDS SERIES

Book 1

The Acrostic of God

·

Book 2

The Acrostic of Jesus

·

Book 3

The Acrostic of Salvation

·

Book 4

The Acrostic of Scripture

Forthcoming 2023

·

Book 5

The Acrostic of Bible Memory

Forthcoming 2023

·

A RHYMING SOTERIOLOGY FOR KIDS

THE
ACROSTIC
OF
SALVATION

JONATHAN GIBSON & TIMOTHY BRINDLE

ILLUSTRATED BY
C. S. FRITZ

New
Growth
Press

New Growth Press, Greensboro, NC 27401
Text Copyright © 2022 by Jonathan Gibson and Timothy Brindle
Illustration Copyright © 2022 by C. S. Fritz

Cover/Interior Design and Typesetting: Trish Mahoney, themahoney.com
Cover/Interior illustrations: C. S. Fritz
Art typeset in Cinder by Fort Foundry

ISBN: 978-1-64507-206-5
Library of Congress Control Number: 2021937301

Printed in India

29 28 27 26 25 24 23 22   1 2 3 4 5

The Acrostic Theology for Kids Series

"And these words that I command you today shall be on your heart. You shall teach them diligently to your children, and shall talk of them when you sit in your house, and when you walk by the way, and when you lie down, and when you rise." Deuteronomy 6:6–7

The inspiration behind these acrostic books comes from John Calvin, the Genevan Reformer. In 1542, Calvin simplified his Catechism for the Genevan Church (1537) so that children could better understand and memorize the essential truths of the Christian Faith. It was entitled *The French ABCs*.

These acrostic books are not strictly catechetical (questions and answers), but they are written in that same tradition of instruction. As such, they are a means of planting the good seed of God's Word into the hearts of children, so that they might grow in the grace and knowledge of the Lord Jesus. We hope the new element of an acrostic poem set to rhyme may help the truths about God (theology), Jesus (Christology), salvation (soteriology), and Scripture (Biblical theology) to stick a little bit better. The books may be read in one sitting (either by parent/teacher or child) or they may be used for family devotions, taking one letter per day for families to meditate on, with some accompanying Bible verses.

We are praying that this series will be used by the Spirit to allow children and parents to grow in the knowledge of God and thus to love and trust him more. Enjoy!

Jonny Gibson and Timothy Brindle

See back of book for more information about how to use this book with children. Use the QR code to hear Timothy Brindle read aloud *The Acrostic of Salvation* in rap style. To purchase *The Acrostic of Salvation* music album, visit www.timothybrindleministries.com.

Dedication

For my godchildren, Jonathan and Adelaide
(Jonny)

And for the children at Olive Street Presbyterian Church
(Timothy)

". . . from childhood you have been acquainted with
the sacred writings, which are able to make you
wise for salvation through faith in Christ Jesus."
2 Timothy 3:15

PROLOGUE

Let's read the acrostic of *salvation*
For Jesus and his work to be our *foundation*.
We'll read it, rap it, we will *sing it—it's fun*!
Till Jesus comes back and his *kingdom has come*.

An acrostic poem uses the *alphabet*
To teach you God's truth, so you will *not forge*t.
God does this in Scripture, like Psalm *One Nineteen*;
In Lamentations, he has a *fun rhyme scheme*.
So, from now on, we'll use the *first letter*
To help us learn Jesus's *work better*.
Here's the work of our salvation, from A to Z;
Jesus Christ died and then was raised to *make us free*.
Each page has a salvation *word from the Bible*,
So that we praise him and not *worship an idol*.
Jesus came to save us from *idolatry*;
Kids, even you can learn *soteriology*!
Soteriology studies how God *saves us*
From the wrath of God and our sin that *enslaves us*.
So it's not just a bunch of big *words for our head*,
But how Christ took the curse we *deserve when he bled*.

Let's read the acrostic of *salvation*
For Jesus and his work to be our *foundation*.
We'll read it, rap it, we will *sing it—it's fun*!
Till Jesus comes back and his *kingdom has come*.

Adoption

ADOPTION is being brought into God's *family*;

We were far from God in sin, along with all *humanity*.

So without God the Son, then *Satan is our daddy*;

Like Cain who killed Abel, we were *hating God so badly*.

Adam was God's son, Israel was as *well*,

But as disobedient sons they did *rebel*.

Christ the obedient Son always *loved his Father*;

By faith in God's Son, we become his *son or daughter*.

Romans 8:15 For you did not receive the spirit of slavery to fall back into fear, but you have received the Spirit of **adoption as sons, by whom we cry, "Abba! Father!"**

Galatians 3:26 For in Christ Jesus you are all **sons of God**, through faith.

Baptism

BAPTISM is a sacrament given by *Jesus*;

It's a sign or symbol, pointing to how he *cleans us*.

It's a picture of washing by his *Spirit and his blood*,

Because our sin left a stain more *serious than mud*.

....

Acts 2:38–39 And Peter said to them, "Repent and **be baptized every one of you in the name of Jesus Christ for the forgiveness of your sins**, and you will receive the gift of the Holy Spirit. For the promise is for you and for your children and for all who are far off, everyone whom the Lord our God calls to himself."

Communion

COMMUNION is being brought very *close to the Lord*,

By his body and his blood which were *broken and poured*.

If we trust that he bled when he was *crushed in our stead*,

We can take the sacrament of the *cup and the bread*.

....

1 Corinthians 10:16 The cup of blessing which we bless, is it not a communion of the blood of Christ? The bread which we break, is it not a communion of the body of Christ? (ASV)

DEAD

DEAD in our sins, we were *doomed in our darkness*;

Inside our hearts was like the *tomb of a carcass*.

Christ buried our sins when he was *laid in the grave*;

God raised us up with Jesus, by *grace we are saved*.

....

Ephesians 2:1, 4–6 And you were dead in the trespasses and sins. . . .
But God, being rich in mercy, because of the great love with which
he loved us, **even when we were dead in our trespasses**, made
us alive together with Christ—by grace you have been saved—and
raised us up with him and seated us with him in the heavenly places
in Christ Jesus.

ELECTION

ELECTION—God chose us before he made the *universe*,

But his choice was not based on who is best or *who is worse*.

Without election, Jesus we would *never receive*;

If he didn't choose us, then we would *never believe*.

....

Ephesians 1:4 Even as he chose us in him before the foundation of the world, that we should be holy and blameless before him.

John 15:16 You did not choose me, but I chose you and appointed you that you should go and bear fruit and that your fruit should abide, so that whatever you ask the Father in my name, he may give it to you.

Faith, Forgiven

FAITH is trusting Jesus and not yourself to *save you*,

That he died for your sins and was raised from the *grave too*.

By faith, we're now connected to *Jesus our treasure*;

FORGIVEN and changed in him, he *keeps us forever*.

....

Ephesians 2:8–9 For by grace you have been saved through faith. And this is not your own doing; **it is the gift of God**, not a result of works, so that no one may boast.

1 John 1:9 If we confess our sins, he is faithful and just **to forgive us our sins** and to cleanse us from all unrighteousness.

Glorification

GLORIFICATION—the final part of our *salvation*;

The Father chose us for this before the world's *foundation*.

Glorification will be when Christ returns from *heaven*;

When he'll resurrect the dead bodies of all his *brethren*.

If we die before that, our souls go to *heaven with him*;

Then finally in heaven, we will *never ever sin*!

When he comes back, then we will *see him in his glory*;

In our new body we'll shout, "*Jesus, we adore Thee*!"

....

Romans 8:29–30 For those whom he foreknew he also predestined to be conformed to the image of his Son, in order that he might be the firstborn among many brothers. And those whom he predestined he also called, and those whom he called he also justified, **and those whom he justified he also glorified**.

1 John 3:2 Beloved, we are God's children now, and what we will be has not yet appeared; **but we know that when he appears we shall be like him, because we shall see him as he is**.

HOLY SPIRIT

HOLY SPIRIT—he's the third person of the *Godhead*;

He's God's resurrection power, so Christ is *not dead.*

He takes Christ's salvation and *brings it to us*;

When Christ comes back, he will make us *spring from the dust.*

....

Acts 2:33 Being therefore exalted at the right hand of God, **and having received from the Father the promise of the Holy Spirit,** he has poured out this that you yourselves are seeing and hearing.

INTERCESSION

INTERCESSION—Jesus lives now to *pray for his people*,

Saying, "Father, forgive them for their *ways that are evil*!"

The Father is pleased as Christ *intercedes on our behalf*;

Our High Priest died and then was raised to *appease all his wrath*.

JUSTIFICATION

JUSTIFICATION is a free gift that is *priceless*;

By faith in Christ, God the Judge declares that we're *righteous*.

God crushed his Son for our sins, so now when he *sees us*,

He views us like we lived the perfect life of *Jesus*!

Romans 3:24–26 And are justified by his grace as a gift, through the redemption that is in Christ Jesus, whom God put forward as a propitiation by his blood, to be received by faith. This was to show God's righteousness, because in his divine forbearance he had passed over former sins. It was to show his righteousness at the present time, so that he might be just and the justifier of the one who has faith in Jesus.

KNOWLEDGE

KNOWLEDGE in the Bible is knowing God and *loving him*,

But Adam lost the knowledge of God by *loving sin*.

We can't get it back now by being *students in college*;

But Christ gives it to us when he *renews us in knowledge*.

....

Colossians 3:10 And have put on the new self, which is being renewed in knowledge after the image of its creator.

2 Peter 3:18 But grow in the grace and knowledge of our Lord and Savior Jesus Christ. To him be the glory both now and to the day of eternity. Amen.

LIFE

LIFE was promised to Adam if he *perfectly obeyed*,

But God also threatened him death as the *curse if he strayed*.

Adam would have lived forever if he had *obeyed the Lord*;

But he sinned—now separated from God by the *flaming sword*.

Jesus came to earn the reward of *eternal life*;

He lived perfectly, then died to take the *curse and strife*.

He underwent the flaming sword, then was *raised from the dead*;

Now we live forever by faith in the *Savior who bled*.

....

John 11:25–26 Jesus said to her, "**I am the resurrection and the life. Whoever believes in me, though he die, yet shall he live**, and everyone who lives and believes in me shall never die. Do you believe this?"

Means of Grace

MEANS OF GRACE—these are the things that our God *uses*

To build up his church—Acts 2:42 *proves this*.

Like prayer, fellowship, and the *preaching of the Word*,

And the sacraments help us *see what we have heard*.

Acts 2:42 And they devoted themselves to **the apostles' teaching and the fellowship, to the breaking of bread and the prayers.**

New Creation

NEW CREATION—the life of *heaven has begun*,

For those united to the *resurrected Son*.

Though not yet in heaven with a resurrected *body*,

Born again with new hearts, now we don't want to be *naughty*.

2 Corinthians 5:17 Therefore, if anyone is in Christ, he is a new creation. The old has passed away; behold, the new has come.

Old Man

OLD MAN—we're guilty slaves to sin in *Adam*;

Every single boy or girl, sir or *madam*.

But if you pray, "Lord Jesus, please *rescue me*!"

Then Christ, who is the New Man, will *set you free*!

....

Colossians 3:9–10 Do not lie to one another, **since you have put off the old man with his practices**, and you have put on the new man who is being renewed in knowledge according to the image of his creator. (AT)

Romans 6:6 **Our old man was crucified together with him**, in order that the body of sin would be destroyed, so that we would no longer be slaves to sin. (AT)

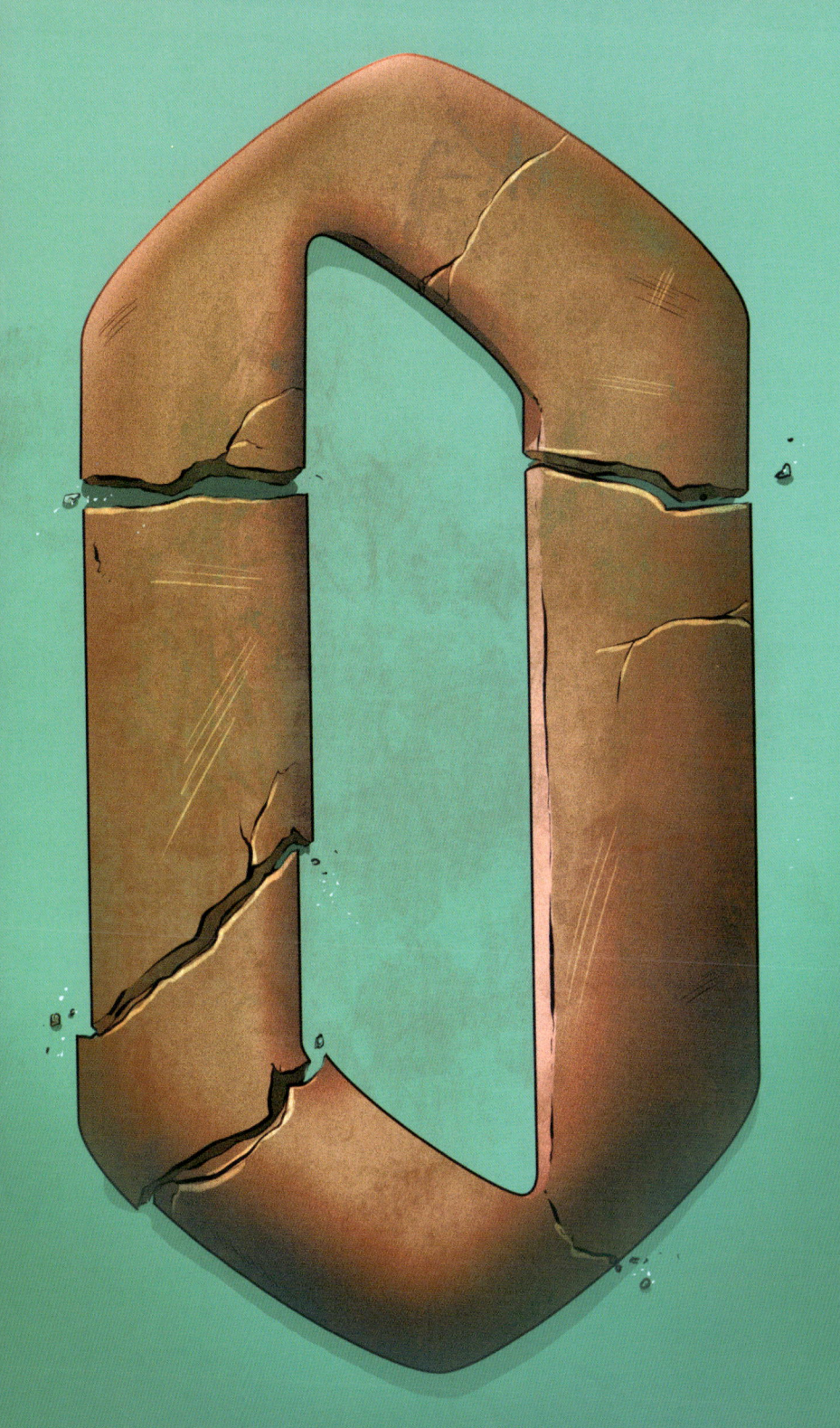

PROPITIATION

PROPITIATION means Christ satisfied the *wrath of God*,

Which is what our sin deserves—we should be *smashed*

by *his rod*,

And thrown in the lake of fire—but Jesus took the *plunge*:

When he died on the cross, he soaked up God's wrath like

a *sponge*.

....

Romans 3:24-25 And are justified by his grace as a gift, through the redemption that is in Christ Jesus, **whom God put forward as a propitiation by his blood**, to be received by faith.

Quietness

QUIETNESS is what the *Spirit of God imparts*;

So instead of worry and *fear, he calms our hearts*.

When we trust our heavenly *Father's in control*,

Then the peace of God will quiet and *guard our soul*.

....

Zephaniah 3:16–17 On that day it shall be said to Jerusalem: "Fear not, O Zion; let not your hands grow weak. The LORD your God is in your midst, a mighty one who will save; he will rejoice over you with gladness; **he will quiet you by his love**; he will exult over you with loud singing.

Philippians 4:6–7 Do not be anxious about anything, but in everything by prayer and supplication with thanksgiving let your requests be made known to God. **And the peace of God, which surpasses all understanding, will guard your hearts and your minds in Christ Jesus.**

Resurrection

RESURRECTION is when Christ was *raised from the dead*;

We too are raised up with him, our *Savior and Head*.

In him, we're rescued from the kingdom of *darkness*;

Jesus was raised as the firstfruits of the *harvest*.

First, we're raised with Christ in *regeneration*;

It's being born again—a heart *renovation*.

When Jesus returns, he'll raise our bodies that are *lifeless*;

Raised from our graves at the resurrection of the *righteous*!

. . . .

1 Corinthians 15:20–22 But in fact **Christ has been raised from the dead**, the firstfruits of those who have fallen asleep. For as by a man came death, **by a man has come also the resurrection of the dead.** For as in Adam all die, **so also in Christ shall all be made alive.**

Titus 3:4–6 But when the goodness and loving kindness of God our Savior appeared, he saved us, not because of works done by us in righteousness, but according to his own mercy, **by the washing of regeneration and renewal of the Holy Spirit**, whom he poured out on us richly through Jesus Christ our Savior.

Sanctification

SANCTIFICATION—our hearts he's *patiently changin'*;

God sets us apart from sin to *praise and obey him.*

We're no longer slaves to sin since the *Lord has freed us*;

The Holy Spirit makes us more and *more like Jesus.*

....

1 Corinthians 1:30–31 And because of him you are in Christ Jesus, **who became to us wisdom from God, righteousness and sanctification and redemption**, so that, as it is written, "Let the one who boasts, boast in the Lord."

1 Thessalonians 4:3–4 For this is the will of God, your sanctification: that you abstain from sexual immorality; that each one of you know how to control his own body in holiness and honor.

Transformed

TRANSFORMED is when the Lord changes what we want
  and *love*;
This change begins in us when we're born from God *above*.
In Christ, the Spirit changes us into his *image*;
The work he started he promises he will *finish*.

....

2 Corinthians 3:18 And we all, with unveiled face, beholding the glory of the Lord, **are being transformed into the same image from one degree of glory to another.** For this comes from the Lord who is the Spirit.

Union with Christ

UNION WITH CHRIST—God sees us in his *Beloved Son*;

Joined to Christ—what he's done counts for us *because we're one*.

In Christ, we have every single heavenly *blessing*;

Yet we get Christ himself, which is really the *best thing*!

....

Ephesians 1:3 Blessed be the God and Father of our Lord Jesus Christ, **who has blessed us in Christ with every spiritual blessing in the heavenly places.**

1 Corinthians 1:9 God is faithful, by whom you were called **into the fellowship of his Son, Jesus Christ our Lord**.

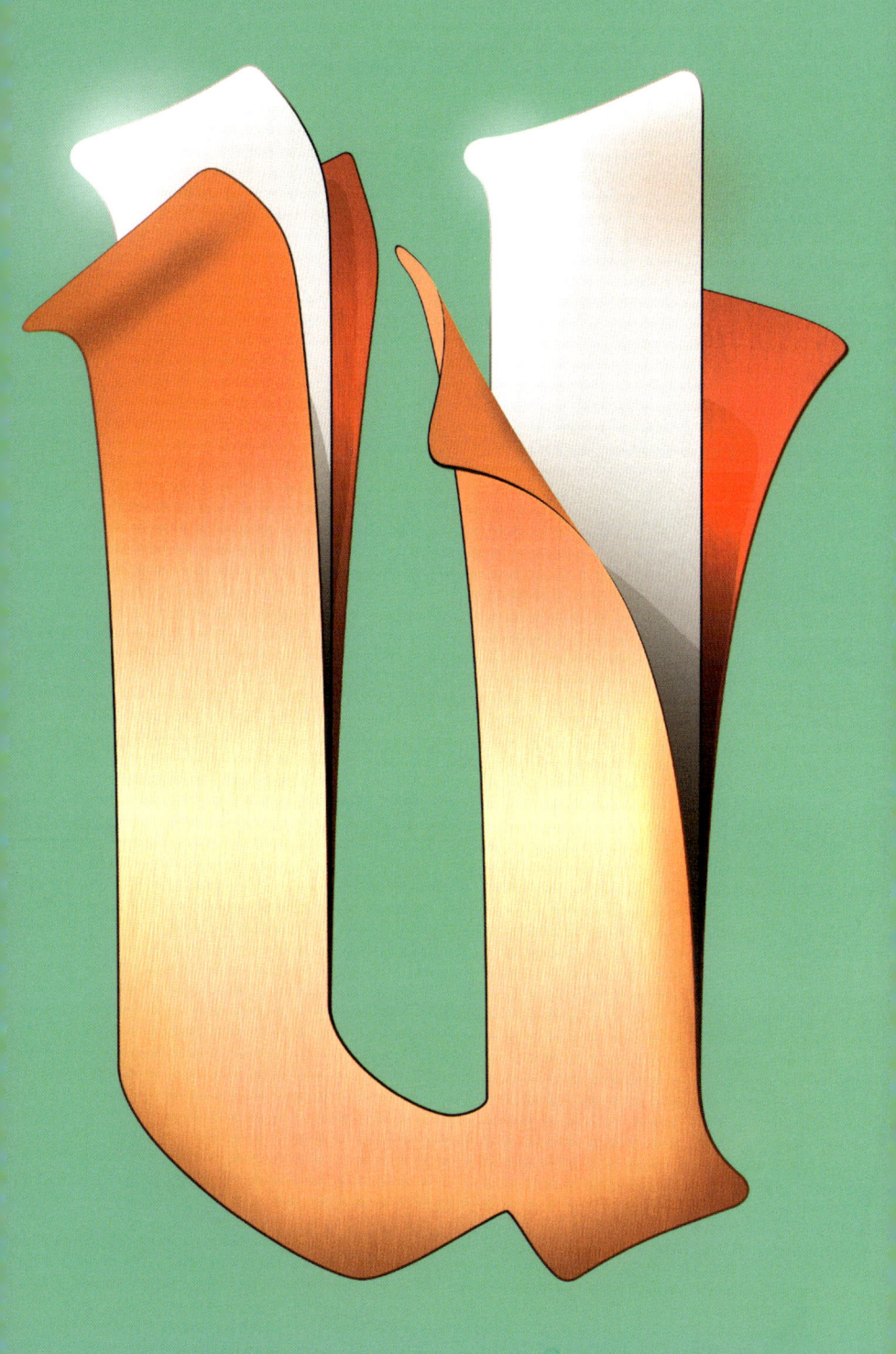

Victorious

VICTORIOUS—since Christ conquered Satan, *death, and sin*;

By faith in Jesus, God guarantees we *get the win*.

Since Christ secured our *salvation in history*,

We're more than conquerors—*faith is the victory*!

....

1 Corinthians 15:54–57 "Death is swallowed up in victory." "O death, where is your victory? O death, where is your sting?" The sting of death is sin, and the power of sin is the law. But thanks be to God, **who gives us the victory through our Lord Jesus Christ**.

1 John 5:4–5 For everyone who has been born of God overcomes the world. And **this is the victory that has overcome the world—our faith**. Who is it that overcomes the world except the one who believes that Jesus is the Son of God?

Wisdom

WISDOM—God says that it's not just about *being smart*;

But it's fearing him with a truly *obedient heart*.

In Christ, we have God's wisdom—*in him, forever blessed*;

All knowledge is hidden in Christ—*wisdom's treasure chest*.

....

Proverbs 1:7 The fear of the LORD is the beginning of knowledge; fools despise wisdom and instruction.

Colossians 2:3 In [Christ] are hidden all the treasures of wisdom and knowledge.

EXPIATION

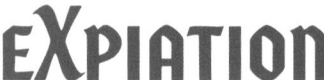

EXPIATION—Israel had an atonement *day*;

It's when the scapegoat carried the people's sin *away*.

This pointed to how Jesus took *away our sin*;

When he died on the cross, all our guilt was *laid on him*.

John 1:29 "Behold, the Lamb of God, who takes away the sin of the world!"

YES!

YES! In Christ, God's promises are Yes and *Amen*!

They're the same promises that he made to *Abram*.

He'll be your God, circumcise your heart with his *Spirit*;

The new heavens and the new earth you'll *inherit*.

....

2 Corinthians 1:20 For all the promises of God find their Yes in him. That is why it is through him that we utter our **Amen** to God for his glory.

ZERO

ZERO is the amount of goodness *that we own*,

To make us righteous before God's *matchless throne*.

Zero is the number of saviors besides *Christ*;

Zero is our sin debt since Jesus paid the *price*!

....

John 19:30 When Jesus had received the sour wine, he said, "**It is finished**," and he bowed his head and gave up his spirit.

Philippians 3:7–8 But whatever gain I had, **I counted as loss for the sake of Christ. Indeed, I count everything as loss** because of the surpassing worth of knowing Christ Jesus my Lord.

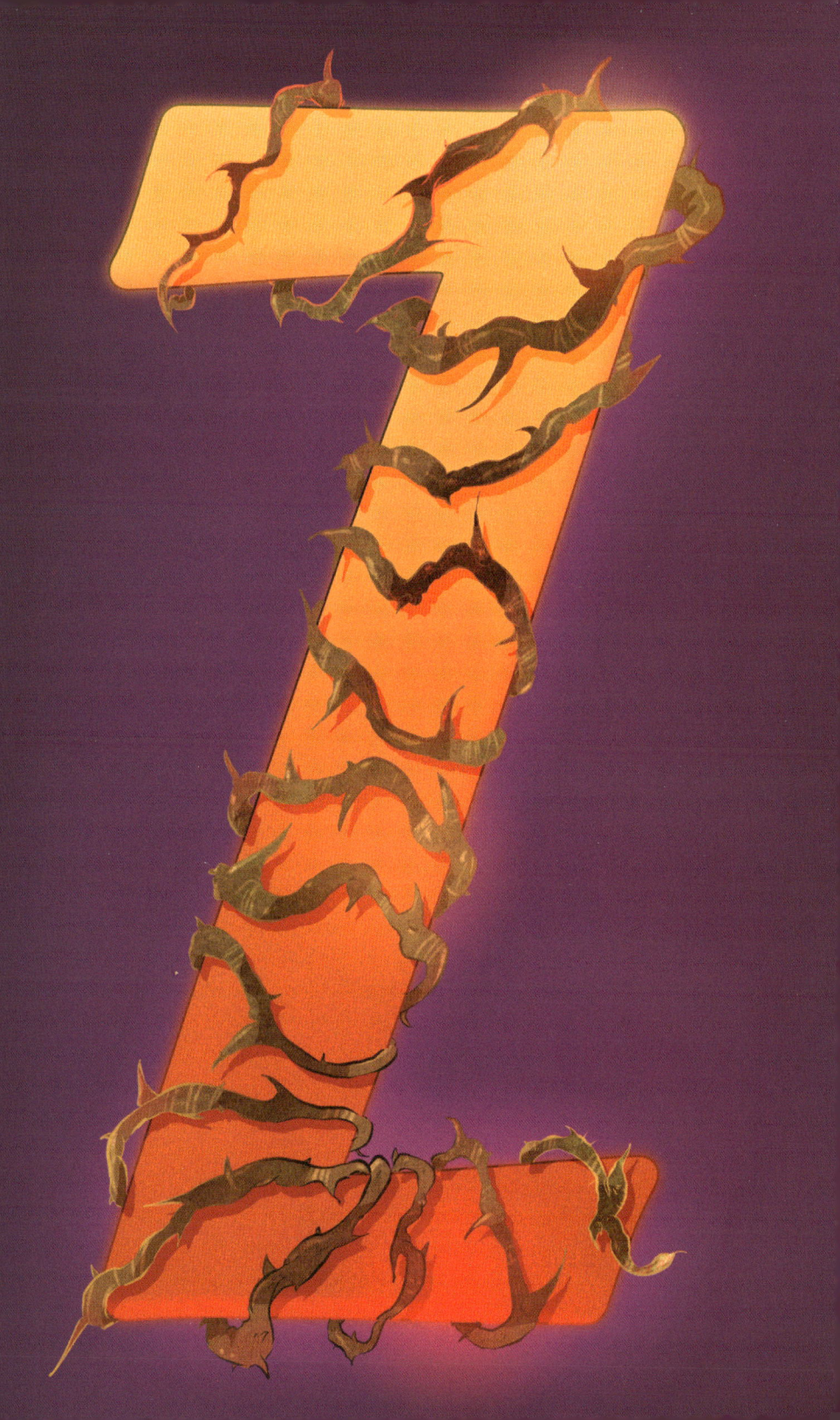

Closing Refrain

Now we've read the acrostic of *salvation*,

Has Jesus saved you from sin, death, *and Satan*?

Say, "Jesus, cover me with your *righteous robes*!"

In heaven, he'll give to you the *brightest clothes*!

RHYME YOUR ACROSTIC

Since the beginning of time, human beings have been using acrostics and rhyme as a teaching tool. Putting ideas into an acrostic rhyme helps children to learn things in a more memorable way than simple rote learning. God, the author of all language, knows this. The Bible is full of poetry. It contains acrostic poems that begin lines with each letter of the Hebrew alphabet (e.g., Psalm 119 and the book of Lamentations); it also contains poems that emphasize rhyme in Hebrew (e.g., Psalms 1 and 2). These poetic features make the content of God's Word easier to remember. Acrostic poems are straightforward, covering each letter of the alphabet, A–Z. The Acrostic Theology for Kids series is written as a rap. Children might be more familiar with this style of rhyme than their parents. If you need some help reading it, there is a QR code at the end of the book that you can scan to hear Timothy Brindle read *The Acrostic of Salvation* in a rap style.

Basic Truths to Memorize with Children

THE LORD'S PRAYER

OUR FATHER in heaven,
hallowed be your name,
your kingdom come,
your will be done,
on earth as it is in heaven.
Give us this day our daily bread;
And forgive us our debts,
as we forgive our debtors.
And lead us not into temptation
but deliver us from evil.
For yours is the kingdom, and the power,
and the glory, forever. Amen.

THE TEN COMMANDMENTS

AND GOD spoke all these words, saying, I am the LORD your God, who brought you out of the land of Egypt, out of the house of slavery.

1. You shall have no other gods before me.

2. You shall not make for yourself a carved image, or any likeness of anything that is in heaven above, or that is in the earth beneath, or that is in the water under the earth.

3. You shall not take the name of the LORD your God in vain, for the LORD will not hold him guiltless who takes his name in vain.

4. Remember the Sabbath day, to keep it holy. Six days you shall labor, and do all your work, but the seventh day is a Sabbath to the LORD your God.

5. Honor your father and your mother, that your days may be long in the land that the LORD your God is giving you.

6. You shall not murder.

7. You shall not commit adultery.

8. You shall not steal.

9. You shall not bear false witness against your neighbor.

10. You shall not covet your neighbor's house; you shall not covet your neighbor's wife, or his male servant, or his female servant, or his ox, or his donkey, or anything that is your neighbor's.

THE APOSTLES' CREED

I BELIEVE in God, the Father Almighty,
    Maker of heaven and earth.

I believe in Jesus Christ, his only-begotten Son, our Lord;
    who was conceived by the Holy Spirit,
    born of the Virgin Mary;
    suffered under Pontius Pilate;
    was crucified, dead, and buried;
    he descended into hell;
    the third day he rose again from the dead;
    he ascended into heaven,
    and sits at the right hand of God the Father Almighty;
    from there he shall come to judge the living and the dead.

I believe in the Holy Spirit;
    the holy catholic Church;
    the communion of saints;
    the forgiveness of sins;
    the resurrection of the body;
    and the life everlasting. Amen.

Scan this QR code to hear Timothy Brindle
read *The Acrostic of Salvation* in a rap style.
To purchase *The Acrostic of Salvation* music
album, visit www.timothybrindleministries.com.